THE CHRISTMAS STORY

from the

GOSPEL ACCORDING *to* ST. LUKE

from the

KING JAMES BIBLE

illustrated by James Bernardin

HARPERCOLLINSPUBLISHERS

The Christmas Story: *From the Gospel According to St. Luke from the King James Bible*

Illustrations copyright © 2002 by James Bernardin Printed in the U.S.A. All rights reserved. www.harperchildrens.com

Library of Congress Cataloging-in-Publication Data

Bible. N.T. Luke II, 1–20. English. Authorized. 2002.

The Christmas story : from the Gospel according to St. Luke from the King James Bible/ illustrated by James Bernardin.

p.   cm.

Summary: An illustrated story of the birth of Jesus as told in the Book of Luke.

ISBN 0-06-028882-5

1. Jesus Christ—Nativity—Juvenile literature. [1. Jesus Christ—Nativity. 2. Bible stories—N.T.

3. Christmas.] I. Bernardin, James, ill. II. Title.

BT315 .A3 2002   2001026482

226.4'052034—dc21   CIP

                                                                                                               AC

Typography by Matt Adamec   2 3 4 5 6 7 8 9 10   ❖   First Edition

To my friend Michael Koelsch

—J.B.

And so it was, that,

while they were there,

the days were accomplished

that she should be delivered.

And she brought forth

her firstborn son, and wrapped

him in swaddling clothes,

and laid him in a manger,

because there was no room

for them in the inn.

And Joseph also went up

from Galilee, out of the city

of Nazareth, into Judea

unto the city of David,

which is called Bethlehem,

(because he was of the house

and lineage of David),

To be taxed with Mary

his espoused wife,

being great with child.

And it came to pass

in those days,

that there went out a decree

from Caesar Augustus,

that all the world should be taxed.

And all went to be taxed,

every one into his own city.

And there were in the same country shepherds abiding

in the field, keeping watch over their flock by night.

And lo, the angel of the Lord came upon them,

and the glory of the Lord shone round about them:

and they were sore afraid.

And the angel said unto them,

"Fear not: for, behold, I bring you

good tidings of great joy,

which shall be to all people.

"For unto you is born this day

in the city of David a Saviour,

which is Christ the Lord.

"And this shall be a sign unto you;

Ye shall find the babe wrapped

in swaddling clothes,

lying in a manger."

And suddenly there was

with the angel a multitude

of the heavenly host

praising God, and saying,

"Glory to God in the highest,

and on earth peace,

good will toward men."

And it came to pass,

as the angels were gone away from them

into heaven, the shepherds said one to another,

"Let us now go even unto Bethlehem,

and see this thing which is come to pass,

which the Lord hath made known unto us."

And it came to pass,

as the angels were gone away from them

into heaven, the shepherds said one to another,

"Let us now go even unto Bethlehem,

and see this thing which is come to pass,

which the Lord hath made known unto us."

And they came with haste,

and found Mary, and Joseph,

and the babe lying in a manger.

And when they had seen it,

they made known abroad

the saying which was told

them concerning this child.

And all they that heard it

wondered at those things

which were told them

by the shepherds.

But Mary kept

all these things,

and pondered them

in her heart.

And the shepherds returned,

glorifying and praising God

for all the things that

they had heard and seen,

as it was told unto them.